Heirloom of Agony

A New Theory About Why Happiness Hurts

And What You Can Do About It

Second Edition

Kevin E Meredith

You may contact the author at
kevinemeredith@gmail.com

The First Edition
was published in digital form in 2014

This Second Edition
was printed in the United States of America

ISBN 13: 978-0-9984534-2-2

(v: 2/5/2017)

Book cover design by Scarlett Rugers Design
www.scarlettrugers.com

In particular to the musicians

Table of Contents

Foreword

The human mind and body bristle with inwardly-directed pain infliction mechanisms, in such quantity and with such debilitating intensity that we must ask: Why?

This relatively short book offers a theoretical answer – entirely new, I believe – that lays out the evolutionary purpose of these mechanisms, the extensive evidence of their existence and operation and, most importantly, what we might do about them.

This is, admittedly, a difficult topic. A typical, two-word response when I've shared the idea with friends: "That's dark."

Of course, ignoring the causes of needless human misery because their presence is distressing does nothing for quality of life. Confronting them head on, as this book attempts to do, is the first step toward fighting back, as this book also attempts to do.

Pain from within is for many of us a given, a mysterious aspect of life that can be neither explained nor escaped, so we have resigned ourselves to it.

Tackling what might be the greatest source of human misery, then, makes this not a book of darkness and despair but perhaps the most hopeful book ever written.

While this might be called a philosophical work, outlining as it does a primary challenge of the human condition, the book is at its core a self-help effort, pursuing practical solutions and attempting to answer in a new way ordinary questions people have been asking for ages, perhaps for as long as there have been humans: Why, if my life is going so well, do I feel so horrible? Is there something wrong with me? Why was my first response to my success a debilitating self-doubt? Why does other people's success just make them madder, meaner and more self-destructive?

If you have never experienced unexplainable pain in your life, you might at least find this book an interesting exposition of what could be going on with other people. But if you have suffered from something strange, sudden, mysterious – a gray mood that comes from nowhere, undeserved self-loathing, a biting regret over an insignificant event – I hope you find here solace, and at least a partial cure, the next time you are stricken.

Heirloom of Agony

A New Theory About
Why Happiness Hurts

And What You Can Do About It

Introduction

We have inherited from our forebears 20 square feet of skin, designed to feel agony with every tear, every bump, every burn and scrape. Our guts and stomachs cry out to us in misery over nothing more than the daily task of digestion. Our backs are a regular source of unhappiness, crushing our spirits with mysterious and untreatable aches. Gas, migraines, heartburn, sore throats, arthritis, hangnails, each delivers a unique flavor of pain.

A hundred billion neurons cannot keep us from eating foods that bloat our bellies. A brain capable of performing quadrillions of operations per second can't stop us from closing our fingers in doors.

And then there is the emotional pain, the jealousy, the depression, the worry, shame and regret. We are tormented by past mistakes, fear of the future, what is and what might be. We go out of our way to look for hurt in the words and gestures of strangers, enemies, colleagues, family. We fixate on lovers who will never love us back. We choose spouses who will hurt us like our parents did. We lose and break our treasures. Even sleep can be torment, haunting us with bitter dreams that ensure our days begin in the soft grays of melancholy.

Anxiety, guilt, hunger, discomfort, phobia. Sinuses, teeth, bellies, ears, genitals. There is not a cubic millimeter of our bodies, nor a dark corner of our brains where pain cannot be ordered up on a moment's notice.

No matter how great the absolute quality of life – no matter how comfortable our dwellings, how healthy our bodies, how deep and steady our pleasures from food, sex, the diversions of modern entertainment – most of us dwell in a universe of recurring misery, of quiet desperation punctuated but briefly by small, fleeting doses of relief.

"Everything is amazing right now," quipped comedian Louis CK in 2008, "and nobody's happy."[1]

Why?

Do we really need pain? Do we really need it in the quantities it's dealt to us?

Are pain and unhappiness simply the tools that evolved to keep us on the right path, physically and socially? Or might something else be going on? Might pain serve some less obvious purpose?

This book proposes that the latter is true, that we evolved to suffer for reasons that have nothing to do with effective living in the modern world.

I touched briefly on the theory in *7 Secrets of Happiness Your Brain Doesn't Want You To Know* (2012, 2017), and some of that book is excerpted here, but I have since fleshed the theory out considerably, added evidence and examples, and come to appreciate that this is not an easy concept to grapple with.

It is not a particularly complex idea, and is presented in its entirety in a single sentence on the next page. But it is both counter-intuitive and disturbing, in that it sets out your own mind as your greatest enemy, working in invisible ways to maintain a condition you didn't think was necessary in pursuit of a goal you didn't choose.

The rest of this relatively short book presents the reasons your brain would work this way, the considerable evidence for this system, how the system seems to operate, and a handful of case studies demonstrating its impact on individuals who were kind enough to share their mystified suffering with us.

I'll conclude with ideas for what you can do to protect yourself from the cruel workings of your own mind, by anticipating the pain and refraining from doing the things that trigger it.

Pain is to humans as water is to fish – so common, so ubiquitous we don't question its existence.

It is time to question.

Chapter 1: The Theory of Pain-Driven Emotional Balancing

The human mind has evolved a remarkable and well-documented ability to bring relief during times of pain, stress and deprivation. Pleasure-giving endorphins, released in the brain during orgasm, are also doing their thing during trauma, injury, even strenuous exercise. In times of great suffering, acute stress reaction can shut down the mind altogether, and afterwards, memories of trauma are repressed or forgotten. Most people can tell a story or two from their own lives when, during hardship or tragedy, there was a moment of unexplainable relief, even euphoria.

Little research, if any, has been done on the corollary function, of the brain's infliction of misery during times of happiness. But I will argue in this book that such a mechanism would be useful from an evolutionary perspective, and that the brain does indeed include this feature, as evidenced by its structure, by phenomena noted by therapists and neuroscientists, and by numerous anecdotes.

Let's begin by stating the theory:

In order to maximize reproductive effectiveness through emotional balance, the human mind has evolved mechanisms that counter excessive happiness with artificial pain, when natural pain is unavailable.

In less formal terms, there is a part of your mind that actively monitors your conscious emotions to make sure you don't get too happy, or stay that way too long. In the event you are threatened by excessive happiness and there is no natural occurrence of pain to bring you back down to earth, your mind itself reduces your happiness with one or more of the many artificial pains at its disposal.

(Artificial pain is defined here as pain that has no recognizable proximate cause, e.g. injury, insult, loss, but instead seems to have been generated spontaneously or is an obvious overreaction to a stimulus)

If true or even possibly true, the importance of this theory to the science of happiness cannot be overstated.

If economists discovered that a certain portion of every individual's money was automatically destroyed, with the wealthiest people losing the most, such would become a central tenet of economic theory. If physicists discovered that some or all of a collection of matter disappeared once too much of it had accumulated, all further work in the material sciences would have to take that principle into account. And if the case can be made that excessive happiness provokes the application of pain from within the mind itself, we must redefine the pursuit of happiness.

Indeed, given that people are at their core happiness-maximizing beings, this is an idea that fundamentally redefines not only the pursuit of happiness, but ultimately, what it means to be human.

Your pursuit of happiness is an illusion, the disguise your mind wears to conceal its true objective, emotional balance, a state so important it will impose intolerable suffering rather than let you get off course.

Most of us cling to the notions that we were created or evolved to be happy, that our happiness is mostly under our control, and if we would just work a little harder or get a little luckier or make it to that next achievement, we would at last arrive at that place where joy becomes reliably stable, if not perpetual.

Believing such things will not make the challenges of happiness go away, and in fact aggravates the difficulties in many lives, particularly when a great achievement or blessing that should generate happiness instead provokes a counterattack of misery and, often enough, bewildered despair. From a 2009 article in *The New Yorker*:

> A young filmmaker named Ricardo Costa . . . recently completed a short film (in which) he stands near the Astor Place subway stop (in New York City) with a camera and polls passersby. "I asked . . . are you happy. . . ? Some people said, 'I think so,' but they were not sure. Some people said that they didn't ask themselves the question, because they were afraid of the answer." The majority of New Yorkers told him, "Happiness doesn't exist."[2]

A similar, more scholarly take on the same thing was offered by evolutionary biologist Randolph Nesse in 2004:

> The triumph of technology over most of the specific causes of human suffering is nothing short of miraculous. But the deeper hope that this would lead to general happiness is not only unfulfilled, it is almost a cruel joke. Even among those who have succeeded beyond measure in getting what people always wanted, vast numbers of people remain deeply unhappy, and many of the rest live lives that feel frantic, meaningless or both. This is the core dilemma of modernity. What we have been doing to increase general happiness is no longer working, and there is no consensus about what we should try next.[3]

Aristotle declared happiness to be "the meaning and the purpose of life, the whole aim and end of human existence." Today, 2,500 years later, happiness continues to elude us. We are too often sad, confused, angry and self-destructive, both individually and as a race. The argument will be made in this book that much of the blame may be ascribed to the brain's evolved self-balancing mechanism.

Why would it be this way? Why would the human mind have evolved with such a feature? Here's a step-by-step argument for its origins and purpose:

1. Evolution favored those born with brains that rewarded them with positive emotions (happiness, generally) for doing that which furthered reproduction, and negative emotions (unhappiness, generally) for doing that which interfered with reproduction.

2. The difficulties of life in the world where our brains evolved meant that the drive to reproduce was never complete. We could always do more, to protect and advance ourselves, to have children, to support the children we already had.

3. The resulting demand that we remain ceaselessly dedicated to reproductive success required that we remain on an emotionally even keel. No matter how much we'd accomplished in the ancient forests of human prehistory, we needed always to do more, and thus to remain maximally sensitive to both the positive and negative emotions spurring us on.

4. Because one is naturally most sensitive to positive and negative emotions at the mid-point, or most neutral place on the emotional spectrum, this place of emotional balance is where one must be maintained, regardless of one's absolute quality of life, recent achievements or latest difficulties.

5. Because the random circumstances of life do not reliably oscillate between positive and negative events, the brain evolved mechanisms to maintain balance from within, including relief during discomfort and an extensive arsenal of physical and emotional pain infliction tools deployed whenever excessive happiness had been detected.

6. Evidence for an internal pain infliction protocol includes documented mechanical features of the brain designed to inflict pain independent of condition, and many examples where pain follows happiness, in individual lives and in statistically significant aggregates.

Elaboration:

Our brains evolved in a desperate, violent world of scarcity, ignorance, fear and uncertainty. Surviving and reproducing in such an environment required that one do just the right things, at all moments, every day. Only those with the strongest incentives for staying on the evolutionary straight and narrow could hope to pass their genes to the next generation. And the strongest incentive was emotion, the constant motivator, the force that makes us cry and laugh, that makes us do what must be done, "the great captain of our lives," as painter Vincent Van Gogh wrote a year before he took his life in a field.

Emotion, it should be added, is for the most part involuntary. We do not choose to be happy when we do the right things. We are automatically assigned mental rewards when we add to status, gain property, find a mate, make love, because these things are key to reproductive success. Nor do we choose pain. Losing a lover, getting kicked out of the cave, suffering insult, all are things that lead to automatic unhappiness, and this is as it must be. If we could choose not to be sad when failing at reproduction, we would lack a central motivation to reproduce, we would accordingly produce fewer or no offspring, and our genes would die with us.

"(N)atural selection never promised us a rose garden," asserted Robert Wright in *The Moral Animal*. "It doesn't 'want' us to be happy. It 'wants' us to be genetically prolific.[4]"

Again, Randolph Nesse:

We were not designed for happiness. Neither were we designed for unhappiness. Happiness . . . is an aspect of a behavioral regulation mechanism shaped by natural selection. . . Natural selection has no goals: it just mindlessly shapes mechanisms, including our capacities for happiness and unhappiness, that tend to lead to behavior that maximizes fitness. Happiness and unhappiness are not ends, they are means.[5]

Human life, from ancient times to now, is a walk between carrots and sticks, our brains rewarding us automatically when we do that which furthers our genes, and punishing us for neglecting our genes' future.

Now, here's the crux of the challenge of the difficult ancient world where our brains evolved: we never, ever arrived. We never, ever completed the pursuit of reproduction. Our mate could die or disappear, our children could die or fall into disrepute, our home could burn or be usurped by a bear. Thus was survival never assured, the quest to maximize offspring never fulfilled, and those whose brains allowed them to rest, to look upon their achievements and marvel for more than a few minutes, were not as fit to evolve as those whose achievements were quickly followed by pain and a new conviction that life really wasn't that great after all, that more must be done.

Occasionally, achievement and blessing was followed quickly by natural pain. The victor, his arms still raised in triumph, looked down and saw that the bear had taken one last swipe across his thigh before he'd been vanquished, or the fight had claimed the life of a comrade, or the indigestion he'd felt all day blossomed in the natural course of things into debilitating pain.

If none of the above happened – and it didn't, often enough, we may assume – his brain lashed out from within. Then came the bitter memory, the anger at a slight or an imagined slight, some new fear, and the smile faded, the arms returned to their sides, and the victor, no longer distracted by happiness, returned to emotional balance, cursed his life and reminded himself that more bears lurked in the woods.

"Perpetual happiness would have led to highly maladaptive, disorganized behaviour," wrote anthropologist

Jerome Barkow in 1997, "the same reaction to a threat as to a friend or mate, the same reaction to a poison as to a food, the same reaction to a barren landscape as to one replete with indicators of food and drink (e.g., trees, flowers, streams or lakes)."

Barkow added, "Perpetual orgasm would have led to a quick demise at the hands of predators, rivals, or simply as a result of dehydration."[6]

A 2005 article in *Time* magazine efficiently summed up recent research on the tendency of people to return to a midpoint on the emotional spectrum after tragedy:

(Happiness researcher David) Lykken proposed the idea that each of us has a happiness set point much like our set point for body weight. No matter what happens in our life – good, bad, spectacular, horrific – we tend to return in short order to our set range . . . (A) substantial body of research documents our tendency to return to the norm. . . Even people who lose the use of their limbs to a devastating accident tend to bounce back, though perhaps not all the way to their base line. One study found that a week after the accident, the injured were severely angry and anxious, but after eight weeks "happiness was their strongest emotion," says (psychologist and happiness researcher Edward) Diener. Psychologists call this adjustment to new circumstances adaptation. "Everyone is surprised by how happy paraplegics can be," says (Nobel prize winning psychologist Daniel) Kahneman. "The reason is that they are not paraplegic full time. They do other things. They enjoy their meals, their friends. They read the news. . ."[7]

The requirement for emotional balancing, then, is a double-edged sword. After terrible events, often enough, we return to pretty much the same state of happiness as before the calamity.

I assert here that the same principle applies, unfortunately, after positive events. In the same way that sorrow wanes, happiness is notoriously hard to hang on to, even if conditions remain delightful. We eventually grow accustomed, even tired, of that which once brought joy, from jokes to songs to lovers. Sudden wealth and celebrity seem in particular to exact a savage toll, the tabloids rife with wealthy, famous, successful people suffering a mysterious agony that only ridiculous excess, drug abuse or, too often, death can alleviate.

Observers long ago noticed what has come to be known as the pleasure paradox, or paradox of hedonism: happiness is best achieved only when it is not pursued. Go after it and you will fail.

"Those only are happy who have their minds fixed on some object other than their own happiness," wrote the philosopher John Stuart Mill in his 1873 *Autobiography*. "Ask yourself whether you are happy, and you cease to be so."

Or, as writer and politician William Bennett put it more recently, "Happiness is like a cat. If you try to coax it or call it, it will avoid you. It will never come. But if you pay no attention to it and go about your business, you'll find it rubbing up against your legs and jumping into your lap."

That we were not evolved to achieve unending bliss, or unending sorrow either, is a given among modern students of the human condition.

That the tools of emotion-balancing include the imposition of artificial pain from within is, to my knowledge, a new idea.

In the next chapter, I'll list the many ways the human brain tortures itself. The list will also serve as a central support of this book's premise. If the brain was not designed to inflict gratuitous, artificial pain on itself, why does it feature so many ways to do so?

Chapter 2: The Mechanisms of Pain

A story recounted by neuroscientist Antonio Damasio reveals the ability – and the staggering power – of the brain to inflict emotional pain from within.

Electrodes had been placed in the brain of a woman with Parkinson's, but one of the electrodes was mistakenly connected to the wrong area. As soon as the electrode was turned on, Damasio writes:

> The patient stopped her ongoing conversation quite abruptly, cast her eyes down and to her right side . . . After a few seconds she suddenly began to cry. Tears flowed and her entire demeanor was one of profound misery. Soon she was sobbing . . . she began talking about how deeply sad she felt, how she had no energies left to go on living in this manner, how hopeless and exhausted she was . . . Her words were quite telling: "I'm fed up with life. . . I no longer wish to live, to see anything. Everything is useless . . . I feel worthless."[8]

The electrode was turned off as soon as the researchers realized their mistake. "About ninety seconds after the current was interrupted the patient's behavior returned to normal." Damasio writes. "The sobbing stopped as abruptly as it had begun."

The story is noteworthy for two reasons: First, nothing had changed in the woman's life that triggered sorrow other than a tiny electric jolt. The misery in this case was entirely a mechanical event, an existential crisis triggered by a misplaced wire. Second, her depression was not at all unusual except for how it was provoked. Most of us have felt hopeless, exhausted, uncertain whether we could go on, and heard similar sentiments from others, and the generator is often as trivial as a little wayward wattage.

Depression, that intrinsically bizarre condition in which the human mind turns on itself, afflicted at least 350 million people around the world in 2012, or almost five percent of all humans, according to the World Health Organization. WHO asserts that the condition is "the leading cause of disability worldwide."[9]

Depression, according to the American Psychiatric Association, inflicts "markedly diminished interest or pleasure in all, or almost all, activities, . . . fatigue, . . . feelings of worthlessness (and) recurrent thoughts of death."[10]

While depression is not the only cause of suicide, it is "without question the most common reason"[11] and is blamed for up to 90 percent of suicides in some studies. Of the 1 million people who end their own lives every year, another 20 million try and fail, WHO reports.

Why, if we are put on this earth to pursue and achieve happiness, would our brains include these devices for such extreme emotional torment?

Richard Dawkins asks the same question about physical torment. "Why the searing agony, an agony that can last for days, and from which the memory may never shake itself free?" he asks in *The Greatest Show on Earth*. "It remains a matter for interesting discussion why it has to be so damned painful."[12]

Acknowledging that he lacks a decisive answer, Dawkins proposes that only the capacity for intolerable suffering is enough to get people to protect their bodies from life-threatening damage.

But the fact that intense physical pain, like the emotional kind the Parkinson's woman suffered, can sometimes crop up spontaneously, suggests there are mechanisms in the mind to create bodily pain out of whole cloth for some purpose other than evolutionary fitness. Pain independent of physical condition is also supported by research. Studies have shown consistently that the experience of pain can be arbitrary, that the brain can block the sensation of pain resulting from physical injury[13] and that – most importantly to our arguments here – pain can occur independent of physical damage. In one study, the mere suggestion of pain to 14 hypnotized subjects triggered the same brain responses that occurred with the real pain caused by a pulsing laser beam.[14]

Research regarding placebos indicates a variation on the feature.

It is generally accepted that a statistically significant number of people are cured by placebos – fake medicines, sham surgeries, bogus procedures and such.

The belief in placebos is so widespread that almost half of doctors in the US surveyed for a 2008 study admitted to prescribing various substances, including over-the-counter painkillers, vitamins, sedatives and antibiotics, with no known relevance to the patient's complaint.[15]

Testing of new medications often includes some percentage of test subjects who receive only placebos, and the treatment will be called a failure if the placebo group gets better at a rate comparable to those taking the actual medication. Recovery in such cases is instead attributed to the mysterious placebo effect, in which the illusion of a cure produces a cure.

The underlying assumption here is fascinating: Some force, which we may safely theorize is the brain, operating secretly from the conscious, knows you are taking a pill and sometimes chooses to make you better because of it, even if the pill is made of sugar.

It's a fascinating possibility, but quite possibly false in all situations except those involving pain.

In a study published in 2001 in *The New England Journal of Medicine,* Asbjorn Hrobjartsson and Peter C. Gotzsche looked at more than 100 clinical studies of various drugs and treatments and found no clear evidence of a placebo effect in any of them except those in which pain was being treated.[16] Studies of placebo effects on a wide variety of pain – back pain, breast pain, knee pain, post-operative pain, the pain of an intravenous needle – typically showed pain reductions regardless what the patient was being given.

"In 27 trials involving the treatment of pain, placebo had a beneficial effect, as indicated by a reduction in the intensity of pain," the authors wrote.

One example of this effect occurred as a byproduct to a recent study on migraines. Researchers used two medicines to block calcitonin gene-related peptide, or CGRP, which is known to cause migraines. Both approaches reduced the days suffered with migraines by over 60 percent. Both studies also included groups of migraine sufferers who received only placebos, and the fake medicines did almost as well as the real thing: Placebos given to one group reduced migraines by 52 percent.[17] The other placebos reduced migraines by 42 percent.[18]

If physical pain can be conjured from the hidden parts of the brain for the purposes of emotional balance, emotional pain should be that much easier for the psyche to manufacture, given that there is no requirement for a tangible pretense.

Insomnia, sexual dysfunction, neurosis, anxiety, obsessive compulsions, nightmares and night terrors, the countless phobias, all are torments that haunt the brain from within, sometimes due to an identifiable physical cause or an obvious earlier trauma, but often enough the result of unknown forces that might be physical or mental malfunctions, or might represent a brain that, from its own perspective, is humming right along.

Aaron T. Beck, the psychiatrist who helped develop cognitive psychology, discovered during years of practice that his patients "experienced streams of negative thoughts that seemed to pop up spontaneously." Beck called these mental events "automatic thoughts" and placed them in three categories: negative ideas about themselves, negative ideas about the world, and negative ideas about the future.[19]

Fear and worry without an identifiable cause is common enough to have its own name: free-floating anxiety, defined as "a generalized, persistent, pervasive fear that is not attributable to any specific object, event, or source."[20]

For the majority of women in their child-bearing years, emotional pain is as consistent a visitor as menstruation. In the days before their period begins, three of four women experience physical and/or emotional pains, including tension or anxiety, depressed mood, crying spells, mood swings, irritability, insomnia, social withdrawal and poor concentration.[21]

Humans have been evolving for hundreds of thousands of years and have developed the ability to speak, to write poetry and use calculus to solve fantastically complex problems. If, in all that time, evolution exhibited no preference for women who were able to pass through their monthly reproductive cycle without pain and sorrow – if in fact evolution seemed to *prefer* women who suffered for a week every month – we must ask why. Was evolution simply unable to solve this problem of pain as a feature of reproduction? Or is the monthly visitation of misery somehow evolutionarily helpful?

Children of a certain age possess a unique ability to impose suffering upon themselves. We have all witnessed the emotional meltdown of a one- or two-year-old who isn't satisfied with life. Because the complaint is almost always trivial, if not hilariously nonsensical, we can dismiss these episodes as the ordinary workings of incomplete brains. But perhaps we should take a second look.

On an Internet search for "kids crying for no good reason," I found a website of pictures of unhappy children with written explanations, presumably from the parent, of what was going on. Among my favorites:

A child lying on the floor, his mouth open in mid-wail: "He doesn't want to go (even though we've repeatedly told him we're not going anywhere)."

A child sitting in the corner, face streaked with tears: "He put himself in time out . . . for no reason."

A girl with her hands over her face in anguish, a plate before her with eggs and two strips of bacon: "We said she couldn't have more bacon."

A girl with her eyes closed and her mouth open in scream: "She found out that I have a name other than 'Mum'."

The logic is desperately flawed, but the tears are real and presumably the pain is as well, and perhaps we should note that human children, like human women, have been evolving for millions of years, and if they all do something, no matter how odd or laughable, there's probably a reason for it that serves survival and reproduction. Might the self-imposed pains of the toddler's mind fulfill some purpose? Practice for a lifetime of the same thing, maybe? Perhaps we are not as different from those screaming toddlers as we might think. We have learned to lament more logical things, and to keep our suffering to ourselves, but in important ways, I believe, we are little different from the child lying on the floor, clutching his stomach, mouth twisted in agony, who, according to his parents, "thought that if he colored himself green he would grow into the Incredible Hulk."

An informal survey of English words for unpleasant feelings turned up about 200 entries, from ashamed, miserable and tense to outraged, envious and embittered. Fewer words were found for pleasant feelings, leading psychology writer David L. Weiner to conclude, "The brain's range of feelings apparently includes far more to punish than to reward us, which probably means that whoever or whatever designed our brains was presumably a strong disciplinarian."[22]

Research indicates the shame we feel after committing a public faux pas is well out of proportion with how we are perceived.[23] We feel that people have condemned us as incompetent dolts when they've done nothing of the sort.

We don't need a study for this. Imagine something dumb you've done in public. Were you drunk, clumsy, immature or awkward? What did you think people thought of you? That you were a laughable failure, a pathetic loser, unworthy of friends or lovers?

Now, imagine witnessing your error as it's committed by someone else. What would you think of that person? That they deserved to be despised and ostracized? Or are you just feeling sorry for him or her? Maybe you barely notice. A quick chuckle and it's gone from your mind.

Similarly, we are more likely to remember the bad than the good, a phenomenon called negativity bias.[24]

From the perspective of evolution, of course, it is better to notice and remember negative things over positive, the thing that will kill or inconvenience you over something that is merely pleasant or makes life a little easier. Taken in aggregate, though, our case is strong that life is both unnecessarily and arbitrarily painful.

To summarize the chapter:

Researchers have uncovered mechanisms in the brain that appear to be meant specifically to impose emotional pain regardless of actual life events.

Emotional pain, particularly in the form of depression, is so prevalent that it leads to close to a million suicides per year worldwide, with 20 times that number of attempts.

The phenomenon of placebos and other research indicates that the sensation of physical pain seems to be applied or withheld independent of physical condition.

The brain has a documented penchant for tormenting us, at any age, with anxieties, negative thoughts and shame well out of proportion to life events or any identifiable objective of propagative efficacy.

So, yes, the brain knows how to hurt us. But, to return to the central premise of this book, does the brain reserve its fiercest torments in response to excess happiness?

Chapter 3: Pain After Pleasure

Your body is well-equipped to force suffering on you, and there are no questions about many of the causes. Injury, disease and other physical problems can cause excruciating bodily pain. Social faux pas, the loss of a loved one, destruction of valuable property, insults that diminish one's social status, these can lead to severe emotional pain, including the long-term suffering known as depression.

But can joy itself lead to a backlash of pain, the infliction of artificial suffering for no reason other than to correct an excess of happiness and return to emotional balance?

There are at least four ways to explore the theory, only one of which will be discussed at length in this chapter. The other three are worth a mention, though, because they are interesting or instructive or both. They are covered briefly here in order of increasing feasibility.

First, we could go back in time or watch ancient recordings to witness the evolutionary stages of the first humans or pre-humans capable of the self-awareness required for sustained joy, and we would focus on those who have achieved a reproductively sufficient condition: those who have a mate, decent shelter and a steady food supply. Do any of them wake up every morning smiling? Do their behaviors suggest they believe they have arrived, their only objective from then on merely maintaining what they've won?

Now, how do they do in competition with their more tormented brothers? When someone else in the tribe achieves something, celebrates and soon thereafter appears to be gripped by a strange pain from somewhere inside, does that second person return more quickly than the first to the urgent chores of reproduction? Do those with the gift of suffering quickly, after a moment of grace, subsequently achieve more, do more, mate more and win against those with the curse of an easy, persistent joy?

If the answer were yes; if, over and over through the eons of our human and pre-human ancestry, those whose happiness was quickly snuffed out by artificial pains succeeded reproductively against those who were allowed to keep on smiling, we may safely assume that we are the children of the former, and our joy-inspired agonies are an unfortunate heirloom.

In a second research method, more feasible than the first but still impossible with today's technology, we would look among the gears and switches and potion jars of the brain itself to watch what happens when things are too good. Is there some accounting mechanism, some collection of neurons that weighs bliss and, when the scale tilts too far on the joyous side, dispatches a pain from its ample quiver? Perhaps the system works a little like our hunger systems, which monitor contents of the gastrointestinal tract, nutrients and acids in the blood, certain hormone levels and such, so that we can be told not just that we're hungry, but how hungry we are and even what we should eat.

Of course, the pain-driven emotional balancing system doesn't have to tell us to go eat pain when it detects too much happiness. Pain is free, a readily available resource within the mind itself, deployable at a moment's notice.

A third research approach, entirely feasible but not yet to my knowledge undertaken, would be an emotional diary in which a significant number of subjects are asked at relatively frequent random times for perhaps a month or two to record their state of mind, with a focus on what they're feeling, good and bad, and the source, if known, for each feeling.

Are the subjects feeling the way they do because something obviously good or bad just happened, e.g. romantic progress, injury, professional advancement, unexpected cash, insult, the reduction of pain through medicine? Or is the good or bad experience entirely from the mind, a pleasant memory or a bitter automatic thought, a sudden pain with no explanation?

And then, how intense are the feelings on a scale, say, of one to 10? And does spontaneous misery seem to follow pleasure in a statistically significant way? The data from such an experiment should establish quickly not just whether there does indeed seem to be a mechanism for internally-generated pain in response to excessive happiness, but also the average time it takes for the mind to lash out, the variation among individuals, and the degree of artificial pain infliction in proportion to preceding happiness. If one pain is abated by medicine or time, furthermore, does another crop up to replace it?

We can't go back in time to see which happiness strategy wins out evolutionarily, we don't yet have the technologies required to know what most of our brain cells are up to, and no one has yet conducted the emotional diary study described above, but we can right now turn to a fourth research option, consulting the large and growing repository of examples where good things are followed by strange pains. In the rest of this chapter, I'll present examples where misery follows happiness for significant populations with significant consistency. In the next chapter, we'll look at a sampling of the instances where strange agonies followed great bliss in individual lives.

Hangover. Grant yourself the happiness of wine and song tonight, and it will hurt tomorrow, typically in direct proportion to how much you imbibed.

Buyer's Remorse. The acquisition of things, particularly major things like a house or car, should be a joyous event but is often followed by pain, in the form of doubt, regret and second thoughts. The malady is common enough that whole fields of marketing are dedicated to understanding and preventing its occurrence among consumers, in order to ensure repeat business. According to numerous studies reviewed by psychologist Tim Kasser in *The High Price of Materialism*, those who focus their lives on the accumulation of money and things – even if these pursuits are successful – report a higher incidence of depression than less materialistic people.[25]

Postpartum Depression. Given that the rules of evolution favor those most inclined toward reproduction, it's no surprise most women are powerfully driven to have children. And, given that there may be a correlation between the achievement of one's dreams and ensuing sorrow, it makes sense perhaps that for a significant number of women, childbirth is followed by depression.

Anywhere from 5 to 25 percent of new mothers suffer from postpartum depression, depending on the study, and because most do not respond to antidepressants, one might guess that the problem runs deeper than a change in hormones or other chemicals. While the incidence of postpartum depression seems to correlate with many other stress factors, ranging from self-esteem issues and lack of spousal support to cigarette smoking and a past history of depression, we might sometimes find the ultimate cause to be the mind itself, acting independently, answering the new mother's happiness with cruel strokes of sorrow.

Paternal postpartum depression also exists and steals the happiness of a comparable number of new fathers, anywhere from 4 to 25 percent.[26 and 27]

The Malady of Modern Civilization. Now, what of large groups who achieve happiness en masse? More specifically, will the modern world, with its conveniences, its pain relievers and its unprecedented freedom from fear and want, provoke a backlash among the minds of some percentage of the newly-blessed populace?

"Worldwide," observed the World Health Organization in 2008, "suicide rates have increased by 60 percent over the last 50 years, and the increase has been particularly marked in developing countries."[28]

A large study of mental illness trends among American high school and college students suggests that depression has risen considerably from the difficult years of the 1930s to the far easier first years of the 21st century.

Jean Twenge and her fellow researchers looked at the scores of almost 80,000 students who took the Minnesota Multiphasic Personality Inventory, or MMPI, from 1938 to 2007, and discovered a marked increase in many areas of mental illness:

Compared to college students in the 1930s and 1940s, recent U.S. college students score more than a standard deviation higher on the F scale (a measure of unusual responses), psychopathic deviation, paranoia, schizophrenia, and hypomania; more than three-fourths of a standard deviation higher on hypochondrasis, depression, psychasthenia, and .45 standard deviation higher on hysteria.[29]

In simpler terms, these findings indicate an increase across the board in mental distress, including a 600 percent increase in depression, from 1 percent of respondents to 6 percent. The number might be even higher, the study noted. "Given that increasing numbers of Americans are taking antidepressants, this data may actually underestimate the increase in psychopathology, as the samples from more recent years probably included more individuals already stabilized by SSRIs and other psychotropic medications."

The researchers considered a variety of possible causes of this phenomenon and proposed that at least part of the blame may be placed on "an increased focus on money, appearance, and status rather than on community and close relationships." Similar conclusions were reached by Randolph Nesse and George Williams, who theorized that modern conditions like the absence of strong kin relationships and constant media portrayals of more attractive people make us sad.[30] But one can't help wondering if our evolved minds, which seem to require balancing pain the way the body needs food, have found something akin to famine in the easy modern world. Making up for the shortfall in natural pain is easy enough of course, just a little tinkering among the neurons to bring forth artificial suffering and ensure that life still hurts sufficiently.

Bipolar Disorder. This condition, in which the sufferer endures swings between depression and a manic state characterized by grandiose plans, promiscuity and elevated self-esteem, might be characterized as the best example of the brain's evolved emotional balancing system run amok.[31] Often, there is no identifiable cause for the mood swings. They are artificial, happening under the direction of brain structures and chemicals that have no need for external stimuli.

Antidepressant Suicide. Does taking antidepressant medications increase the risk of suicide? Some studies say yes, some say no, some aren't sure, and the topic remains controversial and actively contested – no surprise given the corporate and financial interest in the issue: worldwide spending on antidepressants exceeded $10 billion a year in 2013. But for now, all antidepressants sold in the United States must include a "black box" warning that use increases the risk of suicide.

The generally-accepted theory of antidepressant contribution to suicide – if such a causality exists – is that a small number of people are elevated by drugs to a higher capacity for taking action to make things better, and action in some cases happens to be the taking of one's own life. A second possibility, suggested by the ideas of this book is that, for some users, the chemical reduction of depression is deemed unacceptable by the brain, which responds with such a ferocious counterattack of misery that some sufferers are simply overwhelmed.

Plenty more examples may be found on the Internet of sorrows that follow achievement and happiness. Search post doctoral depression, post holiday blues, coital migraine, post tenure blues, the lottery winner's curse, impostor syndrome, and you'll get a slew of links about the mysterious, internally-generated pains that follow success, often by the sufferers themselves. In many cases, the depression and pain seems to be well-earned – a new Ph.D. who can't find a job in her field, for example. But one should ask which came first: did the depression result from underemployment, or did the depression come first, a direct result of the grand achievement of a Ph.D., rendering her too sad to search effectively for a job?

Further research is warranted in all the areas discussed in this chapter, but for now we might fairly conclude that the brain is not simply a machine where successful efforts and favorable life events reliably produce an output of that most important product, happiness. There's something else lurking among the neurons that, again and again, in a plethora of conditions, seems to stymie our desperate quest for joy just as it's at last within reach.

In Conclusion. Each of the instances above, where the human mind seems to respond to increased happiness with the imposition of heightened pain, has generated other explanations and theories.

In addition to those explanations already offered above, some system other than balancing pain might be causing each of the torments above. The hangover has been blamed on a surprisingly wide array of causes, from sleep deprivation and dehydration to metabolic acidosis. Buyer's remorse might always reflect the natural reevaluation that takes place after something someone is just considering turns into a full commitment. Only with an examination of the electro-chemical dynamics among individual neurons and synapses can we determine which sufferers are undergoing a normal process of logical reconsideration, or a common accident among the chemicals, and which are specifically the victims of a happiness meter that reached the red end of the gauge and responded with headache, pangs of anxiety and self-doubt, spontaneous depression and all the other unpleasantries of a mind that is strangely expert at applying them.

There is a more general instance, as yet unnamed by science, for the malady of a sorrow that follows success, wealth and other forms of what should be happiness-generating stimuli. In the next chapter, we'll take a look at individual lives, followed by what we might learn from the ways the sufferers coped.

Chapter 4: The Agony-Haunted Victors

Abraham Lincoln, born into poverty but gifted with a driving ambition and deep intelligence, taught himself law, entered politics and went on to become the 16th president of the United States in 1861.

Despite his success, he was not a happy man. He suffered on and off all his days from what today we would call chronic depression.

Did his suffering increase in proportion to his success? In at least one episode, depression came when his happiness should have burned brightest. As recounted by Joshua Wolf Shenk in *The Atlantic*:

> When Abraham Lincoln came to the stage of the 1860 state Republican convention in Decatur, Illinois, the crowd roared in approval. Men threw hats and canes into the air, shaking the hall so much that the awning over the stage collapsed . . . Fifty-one years old, Lincoln was at the peak of his political career, with momentum that would soon sweep him to the nomination of the national party and then to the White House. Yet to the convention audience Lincoln didn't seem euphoric, or triumphant, or even pleased. . . (S)aid a man . . . observing from the convention floor, "I then thought him one of the most diffident and worst plagued men I ever saw." The next day . . . the lieutenant governor of Illinois, William J. Bross, . . . saw Lincoln sitting alone at the end of the hall, his head bowed, his gangly arms bent at the elbows,

his hands pressed to his face. As Bross approached, Lincoln noticed him and said, "I'm not very well." Lincoln's look at that moment — the classic image of gloom – was familiar to everyone who knew him well.[32]

Once you start looking for such stories, you find then everywhere, in histories, magazine articles, autobiographies, even the Bible, where the juxtaposition of happy event and ill humor is duly recorded but otherwise unremarked – like a Medieval observer noting bubonic death in one sentence and, without further remark, the proliferation of rats in the next.

In his biography of John Quincy Adams, Paul C. Nagel recalls that the sixth president of the United States, when he was 20 and suffering from mild depression, "decided after a year of legal study to have a holiday in the summer of 1788." During his break he received what was surely one of the highest honors available to a young man at that time: "an invitation from Harvard's chapter of Phi Beta Kappa to deliver its anniversary oration."

Adams' speech was received by an unusually large audience, including Massachusetts Governor John Hancock, Nagel notes, adding, "His talk concluded, Adams lost his struggle against melancholy and sank into full-fledged clinical depression."[33]

His despondency lasted until spring of the next year and rendered him unable to study or work.

An article in *The New Yorker* about biologist Tyrone Hayes and his long fight to ban the agricultural herbicide atrazine reported that "Hayes had been promoted from associate to full professor in 2003, an achievement that had sent him into a mild depression."[34] Three pages later, the idea is revisited, as a joke. "When I asked (Hayes) what he would do if the E.P.A., which is conducting another review of the safety of atrazine this year, were to ban the herbicide, he joked, 'I'd probably get depressed again.'"

Pop singer Lana Del Rey struggled to make it in the music industry for six years: albums were produced, failed and were pulled off the market; she lived for a time in a trailer park and focused on working with homeless people and drug addicts.

Initial success came in 2011, with recognition for her songs and regular tours.

In that same year, she came down with something, a sorrow or some other illness that led her to tears sometimes during performances. Asked about a 2013 concert where she was filmed crying, she said, "I'd been sick on tour for about two years with this medical anomaly that doctors couldn't figure out. That's a big part of my life: I just feel really sick a lot of the time and can't figure out why." She added, "It's just heavy performing for people who really care about you, and you don't really care that much about yourself sometimes."[35]

In a June 2014 interview with *The New York Times*, she said, "I love the idea that it'll all be over. It's just a relief, really. I'm scared to die, but I want to die."[36]

Stephen King was a high school teacher, part-time laundry worker and father of two who was barely making ends meet when, in 1973, he received a $400,000 check from Doubleday for the paperback rights to his novel, *Carrie*. According to his 2000 memoir *On Writing*, that check was followed by 15 years of depression (which, it should be noted, he blamed on the death of his mother that same year), drinking and drug abuse, punctuated with the recurring fear that he would hurt his children.

Buried in a September 2016 *New Yorker* article about a woman who suddenly developed a medically-unexplainable condition in which any light – sunlight, fluorescents, incandescent – caused an unbearable burning sensation on her skin: "All this happened to me just at the point when I'd met Pete (her future husband). I'd bought a flat. My job was going well."[37]

The philosopher Friedrich Nietzsche, a few months after significant improvements in his life (a recurring illness had abated and he sensed growing acceptance of his work) suffered a breakdown of unknown cause in the streets of Turin, in January 1889. He was found by the police, according to a perhaps apocryphal account, clinging in despair to the neck of a horse.

Shirley Jackson published *We Have Always Lived in the Castle* in 1962. It has been called her best work, her masterpiece, and it was named one of year's 10 best novels by Time Magazine. As The New Yorker recounts: "Shortly after (the novel's publication) Jackson suffered a nervous breakdown and a prolonged bout of acute agoraphobia that prevented her going outside for half a year . . . It took her two years to recover completely, during which time she was unable to write."[38]

Let's keep going:

M. Scott Peck. Born in 1936, M. Scott Peck was a psychiatrist who, as he practiced, began composing a philosophy of life and spirituality that he wrapped up in a book entitled *The Road Less Traveled*. The book, published in 1978, received little attention at first, but Peck was determined to see his ideas succeed and he promoted the work through extensive traveling and speaking.

Unfortunately for his mental health, Peck's efforts paid off, and as he neared his 50th birthday in the early 1980s, he arrived at a new place of joy. He had money, fame and, he admits, plenty of extramarital sex. In his 1997 book *In Search of Stones*, Peck recalled his life as a popular speaker, receiving "substantial lecture fees" as he dallied about the nation.

Simultaneously, Peck notes, the beauty of nature "was no longer the turn-on it had once been . . . great meals also ceased to be a turn-on . . . In short order, great art similarly became unimportant."[39] And then, he wrote:

> By 1984, my increasing fame had shifted from being an excitement to a burden. It felt like a trap. And soon even beautiful women stopped looking so glamorous. Along about this time I began to feel depressed. It's hard to put one foot in front of another when nothing turns you on anymore.[40]

Perhaps Peck's brain chemistry had undergone a natural change as he aged, or something was bothering him that he wasn't aware of.

Or perhaps his mind, observing with alarm that extraordinary happiness was disrupting Peck's evolved and carefully maintained emotional balance, launched a counterattack.

Peck of course had no idea where the pain came from and remained mystified by the whole affair. But in his words we can detect the iron fist of the cruel being who lurks behind the curtain of every human conscious:

> In the autumn of 1986 it felt like I was dying. Not physically dying – that I would have welcomed. It felt more like being in the Garden on the eve of my crucifixion, except that's an exaggeration. I wasn't sweating blood. I was, however, frightened and tearful.[41]

In the midst of his pain, Peck took up the violin, seriously considering a departure from the book-writing field for a move to concert musician. Which brings us to our next case.

Bernard Taupin. One of the most successful songwriters of all time, Bernard Taupin teamed up with Elton John to compose megahits like *Your Song*, *Bennie And The Jets*, *Daniel*, *Goodbye Yellow Brick Road*, and *Rocket Man*.

The success was devastating. From the June 23, 1980 *People* magazine.

> For 13 years Bernie Taupin had been Elton John's lyricist and thus one-half of Britain's most celebrated songwriting team since Lennon & McCartney. But after sharing in the glory . . . Taupin went into an emotional tailspin . . . Hits came so easily that he and Elton dashed off one whole album in 10 days and, says Bernie, "There was nothing to do the rest of the year. I was bored and depressed." . . . Bernie was 27 . . . Meanwhile Taupin's other partnership, a five-year marriage to Maxine Fiebelman, had also broken up. "I had no

straws left to grab onto," he remembers. "So I
turned to the bottle." His bender lasted two
months before a shaken Taupin "mellowed out
and dried out" in Acapulco. He also swore off
music: "I figured that rock 'n' roll had destroyed
me."[42]

Both Taupin and Peck sought to flee from the source of
their success, Taupin away from music, Peck to it. The pain, one
might conclude, came not from music or authorship, but from
success itself.

Pop music is littered with the corpses of successful,
ruined people – Janice Joplin, Jimi Hendrix, Kurt Cobain, Jim
Morrison, Keith Moon, Michael Jackson, Elvis Presley, Amy
Winehouse, Whitney Houston, Ian Curtis, Shannon Hoon – who
took their lives one way or another, often via overdose. We must
wonder if the oft-sudden wealth and fame following years of
deprivation, a pattern particularly common among popular
musicians, triggers such a backlash of misery that death
sometimes becomes almost inevitable, either through overt
suicide or more slowly, though the abuse of drugs, the only thing
strong enough to dull the sharp knives of a mind determined to
restore balance at any cost.

Bruce Springsteen. Born to working-class parents in
New Jersey, with a troubled father who was often unemployed,
Springsteen dedicated himself to music before he turned 10,
began playing in earnest as a teenager and labored in obscurity
and hardship for 10 years before he achieved his first major
success in 1975, with the album *Born to Run*. In the next five
years, he released several more successful albums and had his
first top 10 song with *Hungry Heart* in 1980.

At the same time, as recounted in a July 2012 article in
The New Yorker, Springsteen was

experiencing intervals of depression that were far
more serious than the occasional guilt trip about
being "a rich man in a poor man's shirt," as he
sings in "Better Days." A cloud of crisis hovered as

Springsteen was finishing his acoustic masterpiece "Nebraska," in 1982. He drove from the East Coast to California and then drove straight back. "He was feeling suicidal," Springsteen's friend and biographer Dave Marsh said. "The depression wasn't shocking, per se. He was on a rocket ride, from nothing to something, and now you are getting your ass kissed day and night. You might start to have some inner conflicts about your real self-worth." Extreme wealth . . . did little to chase off the black dog. Springsteen was playing concerts that went nearly four hours, driven, he has said, by "pure fear and self-loathing and self-hatred." He played that long not just to thrill the audience but also to burn himself out. Onstage, he held real life at bay.[43]

The King of Ecclesiastes. The misery that follows success is also ancient, apparently.

Sometime before 250 BC, a wise and wealthy man, possibly Israel's King Solomon, wrote of his experiences with achievement and depression in verse that was eventually added to the Old Testament canon under the title Ecclesiastes.

The writer first describes a happy, successful existence:

I undertook great projects: I built houses for myself and planted vineyards. I made gardens and parks and planted all kinds of fruit trees in them. I made reservoirs to water groves of flourishing trees. I bought male and female slaves and had other slaves who were born in my house. I also owned more herds and flocks than anyone in Jerusalem before me. I amassed silver and gold for myself, and the treasure of kings and provinces. I acquired men and women singers, and a harem as well — the delights of the heart of man. I became greater by far than anyone in Jerusalem before me.

In all this my wisdom stayed with me. I denied myself nothing my eyes desired; I refused my heart no pleasure. My heart took delight in all my work, and this was the reward for all my labor. (Ecclesiastes 2: 4-10)

But then, as with those who would come long after, depression hits our wealthy poet:

Yet when I surveyed all that my hands had done, and what I had toiled to achieve, everything was meaningless, a chasing after the wind; nothing was gained under the sun. . . . So I hated life, because the work that is done under the sun was grievous to me. . . . I hated all the things I had toiled for under the sun, because I must leave them to the one who comes after me. . . . So my heart began to despair over all my toilsome labor under the sun (excerpted from Ecclesiastes 2: 11-20).

A similar sentiment has been attributed to Abd Er-Rahman III, who ruled in the area that became Spain in the 10th century AD:

I have now reigned about 50 years in victory or peace, beloved by my subjects, dreaded by my enemies, and respected by my allies. Riches and honors, power and pleasure, have waited on my call, nor does any earthly blessing appear to have been wanting to my felicity. In this situation, I have diligently numbered the days of pure and genuine happiness which have fallen to my lot. They amount to fourteen.

Wealth, power, sex – and then sorrow. What a dilemma is human existence. Fire, the wheel, and the futility of arriving at perpetual happiness through success and acquisition all were discovered long ago. Fortunately for human progress, only the third of these has been forgotten and ignored, over and over again.

Myself. I have a vested interest in helping this book succeed by putting the best case forward for its central idea, so anything I say about my own experiences should be viewed with suspicion. At the same time, saying nothing about my life that supports the theory might also seem questionable. So I'll go ahead and err on the side of confession, in the hope that my own story is both illustrative and, more importantly, suggests that the phenomenon described in this book can occur in a very common life. I have focused on celebrities here because their personal stories are readily available and by definition include a significant transition to stunning arrival. The heirloom of agony has been handed down to all of us, though, not just the rich and famous, and all of us should examine our lives through its warped lens.

In my late 30's, I was at the difficult end of a difficult marriage, with three young sons to feed and a hefty alimony and medical bills to pay. Simultaneously, I went from a frustrating job at a failing Internet firm to no job at all. I was laid off with two week's severance, following that up with sporadic work as a consultant. If I couldn't come up with the money I needed to meet my relentless monthly financial obligations, I was facing bankruptcy, foreclosure and jail.

Around that time, I met a wonderful woman who was in school pursuing a Ph.D. in psychology, but my problems took a steady toll on our relationship until, at last, she eased gently out of my life. I was alone, broke, hopeless and desperate.

And then, slowly, over the next three years, I dug myself out. I found a steady job selling an exceptionally good software application to video game developers, and as the sales picked up, so did my income. I kept in touch with the psychologist, and although she had moved three states away, she stepped cautiously back into my life and we became closer than ever, eventually agreeing to marry. I did go bankrupt but, with my debts behind me, I kept my small house and stayed out of jail. My sons were growing up, getting more independent, becoming men and doing good things.

Life, in short, was better than it ever had been.

And I felt consistently worse than I ever had.

I felt a yawning emptiness inside. I could find no rational reason to go on, nor any emotional reason. The peculiar metaphor I settled on as I pondered my existence was one of those huge stadiums with the fans that blow in air from outside to hold up a fabric roof. All my fans had been turned off, my roof deflated, the arena of my life silent, joyless, lifeless. It wasn't just that I felt I couldn't be happy like other people. Anyone who was happy, or just contented enough to want to keep going, was being fooled, I thought. Not only had I lost happiness; I didn't believe happiness existed.

What did I do? What did John Quincy Adams, or M. Scott Peck, or Bernie Taupin or Bruce Springsteen or the king of Ecclesiastes do? What can anyone do to fight the power that lives in the mind, that uncoils itself and lashes out over nothing more than the small crime of a little too much joy?

Chapter 5: Fighting Back

Are you, like our wealthy Biblical king, comfortable, successful, yet haunted by a strange melancholy?

Have you, like M. Scott Peck, Bernard Taupin or Bruce Springsteen, succeeded grandly and felt soon thereafter a strange, lingering pain?

Have you been wildly cheered by your supporters, as Lincoln was, or honored with an invitation to speak to an esteemed gathering, like Adams, only to wake up the next morning stiff with misery?

Do you do drugs to blunt the knives of a mind that seems to hate you?

Do you get hangovers?

If so, you are not alone, you are not strange, and your sorrow is, as this book posits, the logical, evolved reaction to too much happiness.

In this chapter, we'll take a look at the coping strategies employed by some of our suffering achievers, and then we'll use their stories to help build what is, I believe, the first guide to life based on coping not with failure and hardship, but with the machinations of a mind evolved to prevent excessive happiness.

Abraham Lincoln. For our gloomy 16th president, three lines of coping emerge from Joshua Wolf Shenk's account of Lincoln's depression.

First, Lincoln knew how to enjoy himself. He "told jokes and stories at odd times – he needed the laughs, he said, for his survival."

According to a contemporary observer, Lincoln "sought company, and indulged in fun and hilarity without restraint, or Stint as to time."

Second, Lincoln dedicated himself to hard work, with the desire to, in his words, "accomplish something," to "connect his name with the great events of his generation."

Lincoln's third coping strategy is described this way:

> (Lincoln) gave vent to his melancholy by reading, reciting, and composing poetry that dwelled on themes of death, despair, and human futility. Yet, somewhat in the way that insulin allows diabetics to function without eliminating the root problem, this strategy gave Lincoln relief without taking away his need for it.[44]

Among the poems Lincoln recited was "Mortality," by William Knox, a fourteen-stanza work focusing on death that includes these lines:

> Yea! Hope and despondency, pleasure and pain,
> Are mingled together in sunshine and rain;
> And the smile and the tear, and the song and the dirge,
> Still follow each other, like surge upon surge.

John Quincy Adams. Adams, chosen at the age of 21 to deliver the annual oration to Harvard's Phi Beta Kappa chapter and thereafter rendered by depression inoperable for months, went on to an exceptionally successful career as US secretary of state, president and member of Congress.

We get hints about his cure, taken six months after deep depression set in, from Paul Nagel's biography:

> With the arrival of spring in 1789, Adams decided he was strong enough to make another try at his legal studies. Returning to Newburyport in April, he reopened his books in Theophilius Parson's office and sought the fellowship of friends, male and female. Long walks and playing the flute began to have their former appeal, but the most effective treatment for his lingering melancholy began

when he found himself in love with a beautiful teenager named Mary Frazier.[45]

One might fairly ask why Lincoln and Adams didn't both fall into another devastating round of depression after they'd been elected president – surely a greater achievement than a political rally or a speech. Both men, however, took over during difficult times for the republic, Adams fighting political adversaries throughout his single term, and Lincoln ascending to office just as the nation was about to split in half over the practice of slavery. In other words, there was plenty of natural pain awaiting them in the White House, sparing their brains the trouble of generating the artificial variety.

The King of Ecclesiastes. And what of our Biblical sufferer, the author of Ecclesiastes? After he had enjoyed his wealth and success, and then suffered the despair that seems invariably to follow joy, he reached a place not too different from Peck's: "A man can do nothing better than to eat and drink and find satisfaction in his work," our king observed in Ecclesiastes 2:24.

M. Scott Peck. In the midst of his depression, Peck met with a nun who told him he was experiencing the "dark night of the senses." He recalled this conversation with her:

> "Now what do I do about it?"
> "Nothing."
> *"Nothing?"*
> "Yes, nothing," she answered emphatically. "I can't tell you anything to do. I can only warn you what not to do. That is to try to go back, which some people do by seeking after ever more beautiful women or greater art."
> That made sense to me. "What do I do to go forward?" I asked.
> "Nothing. Just wait."
> "Wait? How long?"

"I have no idea," she replied. "Eventually, you'll come out the other side. It won't be the same as it was. It will feel better than it is now. But not as it was. It will be different, but I can't tell you how long it will take."[46]

Peck continued to suffer for another 18 months before his ordeal finally ended. He wrote:

When it lifted, it was not like it was before. Before, my joy had been the product of external events: a new romance, a new book, a great review, a dramatic stride forward by the foundation with which we worked, an accomplishment of a child. Now my joy, while hardly constant, was purely internal and unrelated to circumstances. Success didn't seem to do much to lift me up, and failure didn't bring me down. Some days, when my life seemed to be going badly and people asked, "How are you doing, Scotty?" I'd answer, "Great, although I've got no idea why."[47]

Perhaps we can solve Peck's riddle.

As they journeyed together over the hard road of his fame and resulting depression, Peck and his mind finally came to terms, and he was at last restored to a stable program of emotional balance. Going forward, he would no longer be allowed unlimited exultation in his achievements, since they were coming too thick and fast for his mind to counter without extreme, life-threatening attacks. But he would also no longer be forced to endure long periods of suffering. Peck's mind, in short, had worked with him to find a new place of balance.

Barnard Taupin. In 1993, Taupin traded in the "palatial mansions" of his earlier life to satisfy a "boyhood dream" with the purchase of "a modest ranch in the Santa Ynez Valley" where he was still living in 2014, according to his website.[48] The website suggests that Taupin, like Peck and the king in Ecclesiastes, found meaning in the simple pleasures of life. His website biography (authored by his wife, Heather) refers to him several times with the humble title "brown dirt cowboy" and notes that he is an "avid reader" who consumes "over 40 books annually, ranging from the classics and American history to biographies of jazz, blues and country pioneers; it is by far his favorite relaxation method." Adds the narrative, "He is also an exceptional cook and loves to host his closest friends and family . . . the brown dirt cowboy's barbecue sauce is blue ribbon worthy."

Bruce Springsteen. For Springsteen, coping with success meant 30 years of therapy, regular exercise, no drugs, and intense concert performances to distract from the pains of living within his own, very successful mind:

> "My issues weren't as obvious as drugs," Springsteen said. "Mine were different, they were quieter—just as problematic, but quieter. With all artists, because of the undertow of history and self-loathing, there is a tremendous push toward self-obliteration that occurs onstage. It's both things: there's a tremendous finding of the self while also an abandonment of the self at the same time. You are free of yourself for those hours; all the voices in your head are gone. Just gone. There's no room for them. There's one voice, the voice you're speaking in."[49]

Springsteen, who described his early love life as "a series of drive-bys" and spent the mid-80s in an unhappy marriage to model and actress Julianne Phillips, settled down with fellow musician Patti Scialfa in 1988. They married in 1991 and had three children.

Myself. Among these greats, both ancient and still living, my own experiences are trivial but, I'd like to think, more relevant to the average person. I wrote in the last chapter about the financial, professional and romantic hardship I passed through in my late 30's, and how, after I'd worked my way out of them, restored my finances and my relationship, I was sadder than ever, strangely empty, devoid of any reason to live.

Looking back, the most important thing I did was, like M. Scott Peck, nothing. I didn't turn to antidepressants, to drink, or to something stronger. My depression was painful but not debilitating, so I was able to continue to live my life, to work steadily, to help my sons become men, to make time with the woman who went on to become my wife. I went to church, maintained friendships, moved to a new home and traveled a little.

And very gradually, imperceptibly, my depression lifted.

Life has continued to improve, but I've reached a new place of balance, not so happy my brain has to pound me down, but deeply contented. I still suffer. I get migraines a few times a month, my sciatica flares up, and I have 50 years of regrets, embarrassments, mistakes, and dumb and hurtful things I've said. The memories raise their ugly heads consistently when I'm having a little too much fun. Whatever. If that's the cost of being alive, I'll pay it.

Like Lincoln, I've also put effort into being part of something bigger than myself, in my case the new philosophies suggested by the modern understanding of the human mind. I've written extensively with no expectation of being heard, but the work itself has given my life purpose, and has turned back on the fans in that once silent, deflated stadium.

A few years after I made it through the worst of my depression, I developed the theory presented in this book, and I have been able to look back through that lens at what I'd been through, and the lesser pains that still haunt me today.

I sometimes think of myself as the happiest, luckiest man in the universe.

Arming Yourself for the Fight

Assuming there is an emotional balancing mechanism in your mind, just waiting to trip you up when you get too much happiness, how can you combat it, or at least learn to live with it?

For the rest of this chapter, I will offer ideas for coping, many taken from the strategies of the successful, tormented people described earlier, and several strategies that are, I believe, entirely new:

Self Awareness. If there is indeed a pain-infliction mechanism that lashes out in response to excessive happiness, simply knowing that it's there is an essential aspect of the cure. The next time an automatic thought springs up, telling you something horrible about your life or your personality or something you've done, ask yourself if the real problem might be that you are too happy. Did you just get a promotion, a raise, recognition, a new lover? Are things going better than they ever have? And are the awful ideas coming in waves at a time in your life when you think you should be constantly happy?

Eventually, if this theory is borne out by further research, an important part of everyone's maturation will be an assessment of their pain dynamics. What forms of happiness seem to spark the fiercest backlash? What forms does the backlash take – a quick stab of regret, strange physical pains or hours or days of depression? How quickly does the pain come, how long does it last, what seems to alleviate it? Do you fight with others more? Do you do things to hurt yourself?

And is there anything you can do to trick your mind into thinking you're suffering more than you are? I find this question to be one of the most intriguing implications of the theory. Is there some way to make the mind think we're suffering when, consciously at least, we're not?

The Little Things. The wisdom, age-old and obvious, is worth revisiting in the context of this book's premise: Never lose the ability to enjoy the simple things, the small pleasures, the sunsets, the wine, the food, friends and lovers – the list is endless on our planet. These were the stuff of happiness for eons as we evolved, so, most likely, our happiness is still inescapably bound to them. Forgetting them in the pursuit of palaces, fame and success, even if such pursuits are successful – indeed, especially if they are successful – is a recipe for emotional disaster.

Practice appreciation. Don't let your brain fool you into thinking that things you once treasured have become worthless.

If you have given up on the little things in pursuit of your great ambitions – if you have failed to exercise your small pleasures muscle, so to speak – you will have nothing to bring relief when you arrive, reach your long-sought land of happiness and trigger a brutal counterattack from within your own mind. There will be nothing to blunt the sharp knives of regret and self-loathing, nothing to force a pause in the relentless depression.

Lincoln told jokes and stories. Adams caroused with friends and took long walks. Taupin cooks. Most of them got married, stayed married and raised children.

Success Inoculation. If you are like most people, you are at least occasionally pursuing something big – a best-selling book, winning the lottery, the corner office, marriage to the love of your life.

What happens if you succeed? How do you keep the wolves of artificial pain at bay? How do you inoculate yourself before the agonies of success make you sick?

First of all, always keep a goal in reserve. If all you ever wanted was the CEO's job, and then you get it, your complete satisfaction may very well be answered by complete devastation, whereas maintaining a little discomfort, the sense that there's yet another mountain you must climb, may convince your mind to turn down the pain a few notches.

Don't, further, pursue obsessively. If your only happiness comes from anticipating the fulfillment of your dream, you are destined for failure – whether or not you get what you want.

Make Your Home Among the Agonies. Earlier, I recommended that you never lose the ability to enjoy the little things. Here, I'll suggest something less obvious: stay comfortable with pain. Suffering well is a talent. Accept it. Revel in it. Pain, often enough, is a precursor to learning and growth, and fighting it at every turn will likely lead to both defeat and a stunted life.

If in fact the physical and emotional pains of everyday existence are an essential ingredient of the human condition, running from them, ignoring them, numbing them with drugs, convincing yourself you're on your way to a life where they are no more, sets you up for a huge disappointment when you stand at the entrance to your earthly Valhalla with a bellyache and the ghosts of failure past.

This advice is perhaps not so strange as it may sound. We humans do have an odd relationship with pain.

Remember Lincoln, who meditated on mortality and sorrow to cope with his depression.

There is a whole genre of literature and drama designed to inflict pain on the audience. They are called tearjerkers today, but the form dates from at least 2,500 years ago, when the Greeks mastered it. They had a name for the moment when the audience was expected to cry: catharsis.

Indeed, the infliction of pain on oneself has a long, colorful history.

Devotees of many faiths over the centuries have imposed every discomfort on their bodies from sleep deprivation and extreme hunger (fasting is a central element of various religions observations, including Christian Lent and Muslim Ramadan), to the use of unpleasant garments (hair shirts, sack cloth), to the employment of various, oft-torturous devices (the cilice and a wide assortment of whips, skewers, flays, rods etc.).

Wrote Paul to the Corinthians, "No, I beat my body and make it my slave so that after I have preached to others, I myself will not be disqualified for the prize." (I Corinthians 9:27)

"Lord, either let me suffer or let me die," prayed St. Teresa of Ávila in the 16th century.

"(S)uffering is the process through which we mature," said Pope Benedict XVI in 2000 (while he was still a cardinal). "Anyone who has inwardly accepted suffering becomes more mature and more understanding of others, becomes more human."[50]

Benedict's immediate predecessor, Pope John Paul, reportedly performed regular self-flagellation with a belt. "As some members of his closest entourage were able to hear with their own ears, Karol Wojtyla flagellated himself both in Poland

and in the Vatican," wrote Msgr. Slawomir Oder, in a 2010 book that presents the evidence in favor of the pope's beatification. "In his closet, among the cassocks, there was a hook holding a particular belt for slacks, which he used as a whip. . ."[51]

Demonstrations of primitive mysticism make we modern people uneasy. Whirling dervishes, shouting prophets, entranced voodoo priestesses and men pushing metal pins through their cheeks are similarly unwelcome in the public sphere, the modern workplace and at most dinner parties.

The mortifiers of flesh have not vanished, however; they have either gone underground, suffering in private, or have found new names and logical justifications for their self torment. Gyms, tracks and roadsides throughout the modern world feature a grimacing, panting citizenry who have found perhaps that better health is the perfect excuse for a little anguish. Some wear t-shirts that celebrate the suffering, as if the fitness that is the alleged goal of self-torment is instead a by-product. "Pain is weakness leaving the body," reads one shirt I've seen during my own time at the gym. "Painfully addicted to iron," reads another. Search the Internet with the phrase "pain gym t-shirt" and you'll find many more: "Train beyond the pain," "Bring the pain," and a whole line of t-shirts for a gym in Bournemouth, UK called House of Pain. No one bothers wearing "No pain no gain" t-shirts anymore. The saying is too cliché to be fashionable.

Another example of self-imposed unpleasantness, from the business world:

> One of (our) top franchisees – who sells more than a million dollars of products and services every year – does, in fact, get up before dawn every day to take a cold shower. Why? He says he does it because a cold shower wakes him up! However, he also says the cold shower is symbolic of winning. He could "wimp out," he explains, and take a comfortable, hot shower, or he could immediately jump in the "winner's circle" by taking a cold shower.[52]

Call it winning, exercise, entertainment, good health or spiritual discipline, but it's all pain, ultimately, sown and reaped by your mind in the same way humans plant and harvest wheat. The crops of unpleasantness are brought in regularly to keep you balanced, to keep you on the straight and narrow path of survival and reproduction, to ensure you always feel fully the next pain or pleasure.

Time. The pain that follows happiness might be fairly compared to the bends, that excruciating affliction that occurs when someone ascends too quickly from deep water. It's usually not fatal, and it goes away with time. Eventually, in the same way that the body gets used to existence on a higher plane without need for medical intervention, the mind adapts on its own to an improved standard of living. Waiting, recommended to Peck by his counselor nun, worked for me as well.

What Not to Do

So, what shouldn't you do when pain follows happiness?

Hedonic Treadmill. Those who gain something, suffer the resulting psychological consequences and answer them with an attempt at more gain are headed inevitably for a collision – with economic reality, the tolerance of other humans, the limits of the earth's resources. And the crash will be that much harder when it comes.

According to numerous studies reviewed by psychologist Tim Kasser in *The High Price of Materialism*, those who focus their lives on the accumulation of money and things – even if these pursuits are successful – report a higher incidence of depression than less materialistic people.[53]

In *Happiness: Lessons From a New Science*, Richard Layard writes of a "happiness syndrome" which forces us onto an endless "hedonic" treadmill of increasing acquisition to maintain the same level of happiness. Writes Layard, ". . . living standards are to some extent like alcohol or drugs (where) you need to keep on having more of it if you want to sustain your happiness."[54]

Self Doubt. Great improvements in life should not be followed by self-loathing, painful thoughts or deep depression, so when they come, the sufferer is justified in thinking something must be wrong upstairs, her brain defective, his chemicals out of whack. Thus, the artificial, post-joy pains are compounded by concern over the fears of a psychology that has gone sideways. Further aggravation may come from the criticism of others, who can't understand how you can possibly be sad after all you've just achieved. The reassurance that pain naturally follows joy for many successful people removes at least that compounding sorrow, if not the underlying discomfort.

Drinking and Drugs. In many tragic human lives, the pains that follow great, sudden achievement seem reducible only through chemical means at a strength not normally prescribed, so the sufferers resort to drink in excessive quantities or, worse, the stuff available only on the street. Addiction is the predictable outcome, followed by increased tolerance and doses that grow so large they eventually kill.

Rush to Meds. Should you get on antidepressants when sorrow and depression follow success and happiness? That's a question between you and your medical and psychological providers, but getting depressed after you've gotten all you ever wanted isn't necessarily proof of defect, and might be an indication your mind is working just as designed. If you aren't actively suicidal or bedridden, alternatives to medications at least worth thinking about are waiting it out, practicing at enjoying the simple things, developing a new goal to work on, and exploring alternative sources of pain.

In Conclusion. If your life is easy, if good things have happened, and if instead of the perpetual happiness you have always sought, your bliss remains inconsistent, even reduced, it's not you. It's probably evolution, applying the rules of emotional balance so you will always be maximally responsive to the rewards and punishments that ensure you are reproducing to your maximum potential.

Here's a brief summary of how to respond:

1.   Be aware – this is normal
2.   Enjoy the little things
3.   Set another worthwhile goal
4.   Accept the pain
5.   Give it time
6.   Don't keep pursuing more of the same
7.   Don't think less of yourself
8.   Approach drugs with caution

You deserve to enjoy life, to get maximum pleasure from the little things, and to revel fully in your great achievements, without being immediately tormented by a proportionate counterattack from your brain's balancing department. If this book helps in some small way in that regard, it's served its purpose.

No matter what you achieve, no matter the heights of your wealth, fame, success, love or happiness, pain will be a regular visitor. Contrarily, of course, even if your life is completely ordinary, or even below the standard most people enjoy, you have very likely experienced the same degree of joy as the wealthiest, the most famous, the most beautiful and loved among us.

We humans have had to do many, many things to win the fight of evolution, and pain and pleasure have long been the principal tools directing these behaviors. Enjoy the pleasure, endure the pain. No matter who you are, this is quite likely your inescapable lot in life.

You will never arrive. You will never arrive. Instead, you will continue to wander from bliss to pain and back again. But you will know, and in knowledge is profound power and, often enough, profound happiness.

Epilogue: The Big Picture, and a Little Philosophy

Can it be true that happiness, that thing our brains force us to seek all the hours of all our days, and even into our dreams;

that thing that we will kill for, die for, poison our minds and bodies for a few moments of;

can it be true that the happiness our brains are designed to seek is not only difficult to achieve and hang on to, but is also designed by those same brains to self-destruct upon reaching its pre-ordained limit?

Can it be true, further, that the limit of happiness was set distressingly low in the jungles of fear and deprivation where evolution shaped us?

If so, we may fairly conclude that we at last know the punch line to the joke the universe began telling 13.4 billion years ago.

The joke is about happiness. And the punch line is us.

We have cried an ocean of tears as the joke played out. Now, briefly, we may laugh.

And then, I propose, we heckle.

The issue isn't just your life. It's everyone's lives at stake here, and our future as a race as well. Unhappy people tend to make other people unhappy. They get drunk, take drugs and crash things into other things. People who have achieved greatly and don't understand why life still hurts are particularly unhappy. People for whom their life's goal has been the acquisition of great power, and who are nevertheless miserable, are not only sad but also uniquely dangerous.

"Poor man wanna be rich," warned Bruce Springsteen in *Badlands*, "Rich man wanna be king. And a king ain't satisfied, 'till he rules everything."

When you realize that happiness is not your entitlement, and it will never be perpetual, that it is instead an accident, an occasional gift from the evolved stardust that is your mind and body, you have embarked on a philosophy beyond the ken of the wisest heads in history.

Our brains, yours and mine, were designed by evolution to be a prison, staffed with merciless guards strictly enforcing primitive, ancient rules through the application of rewards (sometimes) and punishments (often). New rewards and punishments don't work while we're already being rewarded and punished, so both are kept brief with emotional balancing tools: after punishment, relief; after a reward, pain.

Unlike a real prison of fences and bars, however, this prison requires your collusion to work as designed. Ask the guards to take you to the warden, and they will hand you a mirror.

For the prison to work, you must buy into the illusion that perpetual happiness can be achieved if only you will try a little harder, get a little more stuff, kill one more bear.

Walking away from the illusion, coping bravely with the knowledge that you will never arrive, is the only choice that makes sense, and it is freedom. With that awareness, your prison yields occasionally to an amusement park, equipped with the many delights of modern life – entertainment, literature, travel, diverse friendships – as well as many more common pleasures, denigrated by a conscious deluded into thinking it must not settle for anything less than everything.

Knowing, mere knowing, has always been humanity's best weapon.

Acknowledge the limits of happiness, the reason it was created, and the value it offers us now despite its tortured history, and the joke collapses on itself.

Exit the universe, heckled off the stage.

Notes

[1] Szekely, Louis, aka Louis CK. Conversation on Conan O'Brien, Oct. 3, 2008.

[2] Widdicombe, Lizzie, "That's Italian," *The New Yorker,* November 2, 2009, p. 44.

[3] Nesse, Randolph M. "Natural selection and the elusiveness of happiness." The Royal Society. Published online 31 August 2004. P. 1333.

[4] Wright, Robert. *The Moral Animal: Why We Are the Way We Are; The New Science of Evolutionary Psychology.* Vintage Books, 1994. P. 211.

[5] Nesse, Randolph M. "Natural selection and the elusiveness of happiness." The Royal Society. Published online 31 August 2004. P. 1336-37

[6] Barkow, J. H. (1997). Happiness in Evolutionary Perspective. In N. L. Segal, G. E. Weisfeld & C. C. Weisfeld (Eds.), *Uniting Psychology and Biology. Integrative Perspectives on Human Development.* Washington, DC: American Psychological Association. pp. 397-418.

[7] Wallis, Claudia. "HAPPINESS: What Makes the Human heart sing? Researchers are taking a close look. What they've found may surprise you." *Time.* January 17, 2005.

[8] Damasio, Antonio. *Looking for Spinoza: Joy, Sorrow and the Feeling Brain.* Harcourt. 2003. P. 67-68.

[9] Marcus, Marina, et al. "DEPRESSION:A Global Public Health Concern." World Health Organization Department of Mental Health and Substance Abuse. 2012.

[10] American Psychiatric Association. *Diagnostic and Statistical Manual of Mental Disorders*, Fifth Edition. 2013. PP. 160-61

[11] Lickerman, Alex. "The Six Reasons People Attempt Suicide." Psychology Today. April 29, 2010. http://www.psychologytoday.com/blog/happiness-in-world/201004/the-six-reasons-people-attempt-suicide

[12] Dawkins, Richard. The Greatest Show on Earth. Free Press. 2009. pp.393-395.

[13] For example, the gate theory of pain, first proposed here: Melzack R, Wall PD. "Pain mechanisms: a new theory." *Science.* 1965:971–9.

[14] Raij, Tuukka T.; Numminen, Jussi; Närvänen, Sakari; Hiltunen, Jaana; Hari, Riitta.. "Strength of prefrontal activation predicts intensity of suggestion-induced pain." *Human Brain Mapping* vol. 30 issue 9 15 September 2009. p. 2890 - 2897

[15] Tilburt, Jon C.; Emanuel, Ezekiel J.; Kaptchuk, Ted J.; Curlin, Farr A.; Miller, Franklin G. "Prescribing 'placebo treatments': results of national survey of US internists and rheumatologists." BMJ (for*merly the British Medical Journal) October 23, 2008, BMJ 2008;337:a1938.

[16] Hrobjartsson, Asbjorn and Gotzsche, Peter C. "Is the Placebo Powerless? An Analysis of Clinical Trials Comparing Placebo with No Treatment." The New

England Journal of Medicine, May 24, 2001, Number 21, Volume 344:1594-1602.

[17] Goadsby, Peter. Randomized, Double-blind, Placebo-controlled Trial of ALD403: An Anti-CGRP Peptide Antibody in the Prevention of Frequent Episodic Migraine. American Academy of Neurology. Annual Meeting April 26-May 3, 2014.

[18] Dodick, David. CGRP Monoclonal Antibody LY2951742 for the Prevention of Migraine: A Phase 2, Randomized, Double-Blind, Placebo-Controlled Study. American Academy of Neurology. Annual Meeting April 26-May 3, 2014.

[19] From the biography of Aaron T. Beck, posted at www.beckinstitute.org, January 9, 2010.

[20] Mosby's Medical Dictionary, 8th edition. © 2009, Elsevier.

[21] http://www.mayoclinic.org/diseases-conditions/premenstrual-syndrome/basics/symptoms/con-20020003. Accessed April 2014.

[22] Weiner, David L. *Reality Check: What Your Mind Knows, But Isn't Telling You.* Prometheus Books. 2005. P. 73.

[23] Savitsky, K, Epley, N, & Gilovich, T.. "Do others judge us as harshly as we think? Overestimating the impact of our failures, shortcomings, and mishaps." Journal of Personality & Social Psychology, 81 (2001). P. 44-56.

[24] Baumeister, R. F., Bratslavsky, E., Finkenauer, C., & Vohs, K. D. "Bad is stronger than good." Review of General Psychology. 2001, 5. PP 323-370.

[25] Kasser, Tim. *The High Price of Materialism.* Cambridge: MIT Press, 2002.

[26] Kim, Pilyoung; and Swain, James E. "Sad Dads: Paternal Postpartum Depression." Psychiatry MMC. Volume 4, Issue 2. February 2007. P. 36-47.

[27] Paulson, James F.; Bazemore, Sharnail D. "Prenatal and Postpartum Depression in Fathers and Its Association With Maternal Depression: A Meta-analysis." *The Journal of the American Medical Association.* 303(19). 2010. P. 1961-1969.

[28] WHO Statement. "World Suicide Prevention Day 2008; Around one million people die each year by suicide." September 10, 2008

[29] Twenge, J. M, et al., "Birth cohort increases in psychopathology among young Americans, 1938–2007: A crosstemporal meta-analysis of the MMPI." Clinical Psychology Review. 2010 (doi:10.1016/j.cpr.2009.10.005).

[30] Nesse, Randolph M. & Williams, George C. *Why we get sick.* New York: New York Times Books. 1994. P. 220-221.

[31] Barkow, Jerome H., cited elsewhere in this book, deserves credit here for suggesting in a January 2011 email to the author that bipolar disorder might be an example of emotional balancing systems gone awry.

[32] Shenk, Joshua Wolf. "Lincoln's Great Depression." The Atlantic. Oct. 1 2005.

[33] Nagel, Paul C. John Quincy Adams: A Public Life. A Private Life. Alfred A. Knopf. 1997. P. 60.

[34] Aviv, Rachel. "A Valuable Reputation." *The New Yorker.* Feb. 10, 2014. P. 60.

[35] Cooper, Duncan. "Cover Story: Lana Del Rey Is Anyone She Wants to Be." *Fader.* Issue 92. June/July 2014.

[36] Pareles, Jon, "Finding Her Future Looking to the Past; Lana Del Rey Still Stirs Things Up With 'Ultraviolence.'" *The New York Times.* June 12, 2014.

[37] Ceasar, Ed. "Twilight: Why did Anna Lyndsey live for years in the dark?" *The*

New Yorker. September 26, 2016. P. 57.

[38] Heller, Zoe. "The Haunted Mind Of Shirley Jackson: A new biography explores one of the twentieth century's most tortured writers." *The New Yorker.* October 17, 2016.

[39] Peck, M. Scott. *In Search of Stones.* Simon & Schuster Ltd. 1997. p. 98-99.

[40] Peck, M. Scott. *In Search of Stones.* Simon & Schuster Ltd. 1997. p. 99.

[41] Peck, M. Scott. *In Search of Stones.* Simon & Schuster Ltd. 1997. p. 100.

[42] Sheff, David. "Rock's Bernie Taupin Sings His Own Lyrics Now but He Hasn't Written Elton a Dear John." *People Magazine.* June 23, 1980 Vol. 13 No. 25.

[43] Remnick, David. "We Are Alive: Bruce Springsteen at sixty-two." The New Yorker. July 30, 2012.

[44] Shenk, Joshua Wolf. "Lincoln's Great Depression." The Atlantic. Oct. 1 2005.

[45] Nagel, Paul C. John Quincy Adams: A Public Life. A Private Life. Alfred A. Knopf. 1997. P. 62-63.

[46] Peck, M. Scott. *In Search of Stones.* Simon & Schuster Ltd. 1997. p. 99-100.

[47] Peck, M. Scott. *In Search of Stones.* Simon & Schuster Ltd. 1997. p. 100.

[48] Taupin, Heather. "Bernard Taupin: Biography." http://www.berniejtaupin.com/biography.bt. Website accessed April 27, 2014.

[49] Remnick, David. "We Are Alive: Bruce Springsteen at sixty-two." The New Yorker. July 30, 2012.

[50] Pope Benedict XVI; Seewald, Peter; Taylor, Henry (Translator). "God and the World: A Conversation With Peter Seewald." Ignatius Press. 2000.

[51] Oder, Slawomir. "Why He's a Saint: The Real John Paul II According to the Postulator of His Beatification Cause." 2010.

[52] Sandler, David; Hayes, John. "You Can't Teach a Kid to Ride a Bike at a Seminar." Bayhead Publishing, Inc. 2003. P. 210.

[53] Kasser, Tim. The High Price of Materialism. Cambridge: MIT Press, 2002.

[54] Layard, Richard. "Happiness: Lessons From a New Science." Penguin Press, 2005. p. 48.

www.ingramcontent.com/pod-product-compliance
Lightning Source LLC
Chambersburg PA
CBHW060717030426
42337CB00017B/2907